To Hyphenate or Not to Hyphenate

Essay Series 12

Anthony Julian Tamburri

To Hyphenate or Not to Hyphenate

The Italian/American Writer: An *Other* American

Guernica

Montreal, 1991

Antonio D'Alfonso, publisher-editor
Guernica Editions Inc.
P.O. Box 633, Station N.D.G.
Montreal (Quebec), Canada H4A 3R1

Legal Deposit — Third Quarter
National Library of Canada and Bibliothèque nationale du Québec

Canadian Cataloguing in Publication Data

Tamburri, Anthony Julian
To hyphenate or not to hyphenate?: the Italian/American writer: an other American

(Essay series ; 12)
Includes bibliographical references.
ISBN 0-920717-57-8

1. Italian Americans — Ethnic identity.
2. Ethnicity. 3. Biculturalism — United States.
I. Title II. Series: Essay series (Montréal, Quebec) ; 12

E184.A1T34 1991 305.85'1073 C91-090155-4

Table of Contents

Introduction 9

A *ragion d'essere* 10

The Italian/American Heritage 19

The Hyphenate Writer 27

The Non/Anglo/American Scene 32

The Hyphen 44

A Tentative Conclusion 49

Bibliography 53

Index 57

a Paolo,
per cinque lustri d'amicizia

It's 2085, you're walking on a dirt road
in Sicily, you're my blood-
kin, a seventeen-year-old girl . . .
Have you
come from New York to find lost ancestors,
or have you always been here?

Sandra M. Gilbert, "2085"

Two languages, two lands, perhaps two souls . . .
Am I a man or two strange halves of one?

Joseph Tusiani, "Song of the Bicentennial"

Il linguaggio è una legislazione e la lingua ne è il codice. Noi non scorgiamo il potere che è insito nella lingua perché dimentichiamo che ogni lingua è una classificazione e che ogni classificazione è oppressiva. . . .

Roland Barthes, "Lezione"

Introduction

I should state at the outset that I do not necessarily presume to answer this question within the parameters of this essay; mostly because I feel that the main thrust of this essay requires further, extensive dialogue with others involved in similar discourse.[1] Only then, I believe, will a path be furrowed and a certain direction indicated: a step, that is, toward a pluricultural notion with regard to American letters.[2] More importantly, then,

---

[1]Part of this essay stems from an introduction I co-authored with Paolo A. Giordano and Fred L. Gardaphe. I thank them not only for allowing me to incorporate our ideas here but also for a series of animated discussions on this topic. (See "Introduction," in *From the Margin: Writings in Italian Americana.* Edited by Anthony Julian Tamburri, Paolo A. Giordano and Fred L. Gardaphé (West Lafayette, IN: Purdue UP, 1991): 1-11. In like manner, I also owe a debt to Peter Carravetta, Victoria J. R. DeMara, Djelal Kadir, John Kirby, and Philip Wood, who are always willing to lend a discerning ear and offer helpful suggestions. Keith Dickson also deserves a note of gratitude for his later, indispensable comments and suggestions on language and ideology. This essay, finally, is for all who came before us as well as to those who, today, realize that ethnic/racial plurality and a notion of nationality can and should strike an identical chord in the United States.

A much shorter version of this essay was presented at the Charles Darwin Society (Purdue University) and later appeared in *The Italian Journal* 3.5 (1989): 37-42.

[2]With specific regard to Italian/American literature, Helen Barolini deals with this subject in her introduction to *The Dream Book. An Anthology of Writings by Italian American Women* (New York, Schoken, 1985); see, especially,

I would prefer that the question in my title reverberate in the ears and minds of those who will eventually pick up and read any story, poem, or play which might fall into such a category as *Italian Americana*. Again, only then, after these and other such readings, along with further intertextual recall, can one begin to formulate an answer to the question I pose in my title. Equally important, moreover, is the presence of the *slash* for the *hyphen* in the adjectival phrase *Italian American*. The reader will notice that I have decided to *substitute* the slash for the hyphen in phrases such as *Italian American* when used as an adjective, precisely because of its socio/cultural meaning. Such a move is one way of abbreviating, from an ideological

---

the section entitled "Literary Hegemonies and Oversights: The External Blocks": 36-49.

With regard to the Italian writer in the United States (one who writes in Italian, not in English), Paolo Valesio offers a substantive and stimulating discourse in his "The Writer Between Two Worlds: The Italian Writer in the United States," *DIFFERENTIA* 3/4 (Spring/Autumn 1989): 259-76. Gustavo Pérez Firmat, on the other hand, offers an equally cogent exegesis of the bilingual writer (in his case the Cuban American) who, in adopting both languages (at times separately, at other times together in the same text), occupies what he considers the "space between" (21); see his "Spic Chic: Spanglish as Equipment for Living," *The Caribbean Review* 15.3 (Winter 1987): 20ff.

On a more general scale, journals such as *Telos*, *Cultural Critique*, *South Atlantic Quarterly*, and *Left Curve*, to mention a short, disperse list, have already engaged in such an enterprise. In addition, *Modern Fiction Studies* has recently dedicated an issue to "Narratives of Colonial Resistance"; see *MFS* 35.1 (1989), edited by Timothy Brennan.

standpoint, the distance created by the hyphen, that is, the dominant culture's notion of *hyphenate writer*. This becomes apparent in a later section of my essay, where I intend to demontrate that a seemingly neutral diacritical mark such as the hyphen is, instead, an ideologically charged marker.

A ragion d'essere

Ethnic studies in any form or manner—for instance, the use of ethnicity as a major yardstick—do not necessarily constitute the major answer to filling in knowledge gaps that seemingly need filling with regard to what some may consider ethnic myopia in the United States. Nevertheless (by now a cliché), we all know that the United States of America was born and developed—at times with tragic results[3]—along lines of diversity. What is important in this regard is that we understand, or a least *try* to understand, the origins of the diversity and difference which characterize the many ethnic and racial groups that constitute the kaleidoscopic population of our country.

Accepting literature as, among many things, the mirror of the society in which it is conceived, created, and perceived, we come to understand that one of the many questions ethnic literature addresses is the negative stereotypes of members of ethnic/ racial groups which are not part and parcel of the dominant culture.[4] To be sure, one of the

---

[3]Of numerous historical cases, I have in mind the egregious examples of Native Americans and Black Americans.

[4]By ethnic literature, I mean that type of writing which deals, contextually, with customs and behavioral patterns that the North American mindset may consider different from what it perceives as mainstream. The difference, I might add, may also manifest itself formalistically—the writer may

goals of ethnic literature is to dislodge and debunk the negative stereotypes. In turn, through the natural dynamics of intertextual recall and inference, the reader engages in a process of analytical inquiry and comparison of the ethnic group(s) in question with other ethnic groups as well as with the dominant culture. In fact, it is precisely through a comparative process that one comes to understand how difference and diversity from one group to another may not be as great as it initially seems; indeed, that such difference and diversity can not only co-exist but may even overlap with that which is considered characteristic of the dominant group. This, I believe, is another of the goals/functions of ethnic literature: to impart knowledge of the customs, characteristics, and language, of the various racial and ethnic groups in this country. Finally, partial responsibility for the validity or lack thereof of *other* literatures also lies with the *critic* or *theorist*. In fact, the theorist's end goal for *other* literatures, perhaps, should not limit itself only to the invention of another mode of reading. Instead, it should become, in itself, a strategy of reading which extends beyond the limits of textual analysis; it should concomitantly, and

---

not follow what has become accepted norms and conventions of literary creation, s/he may not produce what the dominant culture considers *good* literature.

Of the many questions any literature addresses are those concerned with the aesthetic and artistic dynamics. Not immediate to my essay, I leave them for another time and place.

ultimately, aim for the validation of the text(s) in question vis-à-vis those already validated by the dominant culture.

A cultural situation analogous to that of ethnic literature in the United States is examined by Ketu H. Katrek, in the first section of her acute essay dedicated to postcolonial women's texts. There, she underscores Western intellectuals' unconscious compliance in "validating the dominant power structure, even when they ideologically oppose such hegemonic power."[5] Furthermore, she takes issue with Fredric Jameson, for instance, for not exploring the "historically specific reasons for nationalist ideologies in postcolonial societies," inasmuch as he, according to Katrek, reduces everything to the category of "national allegories," which, as Katrek continues to suggest, casts aside other pertinent categories such as gender, class, race, ethnicity, language, and religion. Germane to any discourse trying to understand how and why some works are canonized and others not are Jameson's opening words:

> Judging from recent conversations among third-world intellectuals, there is now an obsessive return of the national situation itself, the name of the country that returns again and again like a gong, the collective

---

[5]See her "Decolonializing Culture: Toward a Theory for Postcolonial Women's Text," *Modern Fiction Studies* 35.1: 159.

> attention to "us," and what we have to do and how we do it, to what we can't do and what we do better than this or that nationality, or unique characteristics, in short, to the level of "people." *This is not the way American intellectuals have been discussing "America," and indeed one might feel that the whole matter is nothing but that old thing called "nationalism," long since liquidated here and rightly so* (my emphasis).[6]

Before continuing, however, it should be pointed out that Jameson does distance himself from the seemingly ethnocentric and chauvinistic tone to his opening remarks. He sets off America and nationalism in quotation marks; and, furthermore, he continues this opening paragraph by underscoring the fundamentality of nationalism in the third world, thus making it "legitimate to ask whether it is all that bad in the end." Undoubtedly, in a more general context beyond the specificities of Jameson's discourse, these are indeed disturbing words for anyone sympathetic both to colonial resistance, as is Katrek (who, here, unfortunately, has not grasped Jameson's irony), and to other categories of literature which are not necessarily in concert with notions validating, conversely, a dominant culture. For Jameson's ironic engagement in the devil's advocacy, his projection of a sense of willynilly unconscious monoculturalism is

[6]Frederic Jameson, "Third World Literature in an Era of Multinational Capitalism," *Social Text* 15 (1986): 65.

pronounced by his very choice of words such as "America" for United States, where "nationalism" (or, for that matter, any term designating *otherness* may be easily substituted, as was implied above) had long been "liquidated and rightfully so."

Such general ideas offer no opportunity for any sort of intellectual divergence and, thus, makes it further difficult for any sort of marginalized artform to be recognized by the mainstream; in leaving no room for deviation, such ideas are, *de facto,* in disaccord with any sort of notion of pluriculturalism. A case in point is Aijaz Ahmad's response to Jameson's essay.[7] More relevant to my enterprise, however, are not so much the criticisms he brings to Jameson's essay, as his own notions that originated such criticisms. Most significant, indeed, are those points Ahmad raises with regard to the notion of a "third-world" literature, issues—I would contend—analogous to the situation of ethnic literature in the United States. First and foremost, Ahmad states, such a notion cannot be "constructed as an internally coherent object of theoretical knowledge"; that such a categorization "cannot be resolved . . . without an altogether positivist reductionism." Secondly, the "major literary traditions [of the third world] remain, beyond a few

[7] See Aijaz Ahmad's response: "Jameson's Rhetoric of Otherness and the 'National Allegory'," *Social Text* 17 (1987): 3-25.

texts here and there, virtually unknown to the *American* literary theorist" (my emphasis). Finally, "literary texts are produced in highly differentiated, usually overdetermined contexts of *competing ideological and cultural clusters, so that any particular text of any complexity shall always have to be placed within the cluster that gives it its energy and form, before it is totalised into a universal category*" (my emphasis). Thus, it is within this ideological framework that I shall consider further the notion of the seemingly neutral hyphen and its value as not a mere linguistic element but indeed an ideological construct.

The notion for an enterprise of this type is grounded in a slightly unorthodox mode of thought. The very title of my essay—by joining together two terms of an adjectival phrase with a slash and not the traditional hyphen—may clamor loudly inasmuch as it may be considered an affront to grammatical exigencies of the English language.[8] I, however, maintain such a liberty to be valid for reasons which become clear later—some might say grammatical anarchy—precisely because rules and/or usage of grammar are arbitrary constructs set up by those who are

---

[8]By English language, I mean that version spoken within the borders of the United States. I have opted for English over American since the latter term is not necessarily restricted only to the area we recognize as the United States; American, to name a few, are also Canada, Mexico, Argentina, and Brazil.

empowered to do so. My objection, I should state, is not to grammar rules in general; my intentions are not to call for general, grammatical anarchy. However, I do believe that there are cases where the grammar rule/ usage may connote an inherent prejudice, no matter how slight. Besides the hyphen, one example that comes to mind is the usage of the male pronoun for the impersonal, whereas all of its alternatives—*s/he, she/he,* or *he/she*—are shunned. In this poststructuralist, postmodern society in which we live, my essay therefore casts by the wayside any notion of universality or absoluteness with regard to the regulated use of the hyphen in adjectival phrases denoting national origin, ethnicity, race, or gender. Undoubtedly, one can, and should, readily equate the abovementioned notion to some general notions associated with the postmodern. To be sure, the various juxtapositions we now associate with *a* postmodern discourse lie at the base of what I propose in the following pages: stability / subversion; hierarchy / anarchy; determinacy / indeterminacy; genital / polymorphous.

Any rejection of validity of the notion of "hierarchy," or better, universality or absoluteness, is characteristic of those who are, to paraphrase Lyotard, "incredul[ous] toward [grand or] metanarratives."[9] Indeed, one of

---

[9]Jean-François Lyotard, *The Postmodern Condition: A Report on Knowledge*, trans. Geoff Bennington and Brian

the legitimized *and* legitimizing *grand récits*—metanarrative—is the discourse built around the notion of canon valorization. By implicitly constructing an otherwise non-existent category, or *sub*genre, of American letters—Italian/American literature—the notion of a centered canon of the dominant Anglo/American culture is rattled once more. Rattled *once more* precisely because there already exist, fortunately, *legitimized*—that is, considering the Academy the legitimizing institution—similar categories such as African/American or Jewish/American fiction; one need only peruse the list of graduate courses in American and English literature in the various catalogues of major American universities.[10]

Massumi with a foreword by Frederic Jameson (Minneapolis: U Minnesota P, 1984): xiv.

[10]With regard to a discussion around the general notion of canon, I leave that for a larger setting, one which allows more space for such an encompassing argument. For more on the notion of canons, see *Canons*, edited by Robert von Hallberg (Chicago: U Chicago P, 1984); especially Charles Altieri, "An Idea and Ideal of a Literary Canon" and Richard Ohmann, "The Shaping of a Canon: U.S. Fiction, 1960-1975": 41-64, 377-402.

The Italian/American Heritage: From Italian to American and Back Again

Poet and novelist Jay Parini revealed that his second fictional effort, *The Patch Boys*, was a novel of recovery: one in which he had been able to use the Italian elements of his upbringing to tell a story and, in so doing, was able to regain aspects of his heritage, which, for the most part, had been previously ignored or untapped.[11] Parini's recovery of a sense of his own *italianità* is indeed indicative of the sentiment and spirit of today's younger Italian/American writer, such as Tony Ardizzone, Kenny Marotta, Lisa Ruffolo, Diane Raptosh, and Dana Gioia, just to mention a few.[12]

Pertinent to any discourse on ethnic recovery, as in Parini's, is the notion that ethnicity is not a fixed essence passed down from one generation to the next. Rather, "ethnicity is something reinvented and reinterpreted in each generation by each

---

[11] See his interview in *Fra Noi* (April 1987).

[12] My use of the term *italianità* should not be identified with any past, historical Italian usage. I believe we can cleanse it of its Fascist smirches and, as is my intention here and elsewhere, reclaim its original ahistorical meaning of adherence to and/or participation in that which pertains to Italy and Italian culture in general. I would like to thank Paolo Valesio for having underscored this ambiguity.

individual,"[13] which, in the end, is a way of "finding a voice or style that does not violate one's *several components of identity*" (my emphasis), these components constituting the specificities of each individual. Thus, ethnicity—and more specifically in this case, *italianità*—is redefined and reinterpreted on the basis of each individual's time and place, and is therefore always new and different with respect to its own historical specificities vis-à-vis the dominant culture.

We might, then, ask ourselves what exactly is this *italianità* that these and other writers such as Parini are interested in re(dis)-covering? And what lies at the base of their need or desire for such a re(dis)covery? *Italianità* is indeed a term expressive of many notions, ideas, feelings, and sentiments. To be sure, it is any and all of these things which lead young Italian Americans back to their real and mythical images of the land, the way of life, the values and the cultural trappings of their ancestors. It could be language, food, a way of determining life values, a familial structure, a sense of religion; it can be all of these, as it can certainly be much more. Undoubtedly, a polysemic term such as *italianità* evades a precise definition. However, such a cultural concept is possible to

---

[13] Michael M. J. Fischer, "Ethnicity and the Post-Modern Arts of Memory," in *Writing Culture. The Poetics and Politics of Ethnography*. Edited by James Clifford and George E. Marcus (Berkeley; U of California P, 1986): 195.

perceive and ultimately interpret through the evidence found in the large body of Italian/American creative literature.

American writers of Italian descent have obviously contributed greatly to the establishment of an Italian identity in America. Yet few have been able to avoid being relegated to the category of *ethnic* writers, and therefore cast on the margin, as opposed to being considered part of the larger, dominant group we call American writers. The problem here, of course, is that the term *ethnic*, unfortunately, has a negative connotation for those prepossessive of an *American* mindset.[14] Because of this marginalizing phenomenon, many have even avoided direct association with their ethnic heritage at large. This avoidance is sometimes preferred, precisely because too often the literary contributions of American writers of Italian descent have been channelled onto an ethnic side street of American literature. Such *ghettoizing* is exemplified by an incident recounted by the late John Ciardi. He once published a poem in the *Atlantic Monthly* about Italy and Mussolini. The late poet and critic Robert Lowell acknowledged the poem as, according to Ciardi,

---

[14]This is equally true of other ethnic, racial, and sexual groupings. The difference, here, is that they seem to have acquired, and rightfully so, a high cultural currency; Italian/American writers, instead, have yet to do so.

> . . . the best Italian American poem he had ever seen. And I thought, "Does this son of a bitch think he is more American than I am?" Where does he think I was brought up? Because my name is Ciardi, he decided to hyphenate the poem. Had it been a Yankee name, he would have thought, "Ah, a scholar who knows about Italy." Sure he made assumptions, but I can't grant for a minute that Lowell is any more American than I am. . .[15]

To be sure, Ciardi's complaint is one which, until recently, has echoed throughout the careers of many American writers of Italian descent. Perhaps what Lowell and many other critics found in the writings of many Italian Americans such as Ciardi was a strong sense of their cultural heritage (*italianità*)—the writer's notion of self which dominant-group critics had trouble perceiving, if not accepting, as something which could be viably American.

The earliest American writers of Italian descent became, in essence, pioneers of Italian/American self-discovery, definition and declamation. Their writing depicted the struggles, dreams, nightmares, and reality of what it meant to be an American of Italian descent. Not by choice, most of them were restricted to life in "Little Italys," and thus their writing begins with anecdotal accounts of the joys and sorrows—the reality, that is,

---

[15]See, Linda Caetura, ed, *Growing Up Italian* (New York: Morrow & Co., 1985): 150.

of life in these immigrant enclaves. These experiences created a number of obstacles that would challenge the writing abilities of early Italian/American authors. First, there was the need to establish economic security in order to enable the development of a writing discipline: though not impossible, it is indeed difficult to concentrate on one's writing when one must concurrently struggle to secure life's necessities. Secondly, there was the need to acquire the requisite tools of the writer; those whose first language was Italian needed to master English before they could even consider the possibility of contributing to an American literary mosaic. This, then, meant attending American schools, reading American literature, and developing an American identity.

Those writers who managed to achieve these first two goals still faced a third and more difficult obstacle to overcome: the need to enter the publishing world in order to gain access to the American audience. The writers who were able to meet all three of these requirements were few in number; yet their efforts have given us a body of writing we may now consider classic of *italianità* in America. Some writers of Italian descent whose works have endured the test of time are John Fante, Pietro Di Donato, Jerre Mangione in fiction, or Diane di Prima,

Lawrence Ferlinghetti, Felix Stefanile, Joseph Tusiani, and Gregory Corso in poetry.[16]

It is only in retrospect that we can identify the works of these authors as classics or soon-to-become classics. And it is precisely upon this recently established classical basis that a great body of American literature, imbued to a significant degree with *italianità,* has begun to take form and also distinguish itself as a literature which can no longer be relegated to the side streets of American literature. Helen Barolini offered the following explanation as

---

[16]While it is true that these and others have been singled out because of that which distinguishes them from the Anglo/American canon, these are writers whose works, according to Giose Rimanelli, ". . . endure the reflex of time or impose themselves on new generations" (See his introduction to *Modern Canadian Studies* [Toronto: Reyerson Press, 1966]: xiii). Evidence for Rimanelli's statement is, of course, that their works not only remain in print but indeed much has since become the subject of scholarly inquiries; and, in the case of Pietro Di Donato and John Fante, some works served as inspirations for films.

On a more somber note, it is equally important to point out that in these early years there were very few women who engaged in creative writing. As opposed to the figure of the woman writer of the dominant culture, work on the figure of the female Italian/American writer has yet to be greatly explored. To date, to name a few, one may consult, Betty Boyd Caroli, Robert F. Harney, and Lydio F. Tomasi, eds. *The Italian Immigrant Woman in North America* (Toronto: The Multicultural History Society in Ontario, 1978), Helen Barolini, "Introduction," *The Dream Book. An Anthology of Writings by Italian American Women* (New York: Schoken, 1985), and Mary Jo Bona's essay, "Mari Tomasi's *Like Lesser Gods*: The Making of an Ethnic *Bildungsroman*," *Voices in Italian Americana* 1.1 (1990): 15-34.

to why Italian/American literature has not fared better in this country:

> The greatest Italian American literary piece is still *Christ in Concrete.* And perhaps as a female counterpart, the illiterate Rosa Cassettari's story which was written down as oral history by Marie Hall Ets. Both these narratives are autobiographical, although Di Donato's is couched in fictional form. But both leave the brute strength of experience, and it is this experiential mode that denotes both our richness and our burden. It is as though style and linguistic daring is still being sacrificed to the white heat of telling our story . . . only when our history—our story, if you will—has been transcended will we come into our own stylistically and be open to some greater experimentation of theme and style.[17]

This idea of transcending the history in order to present the story is one that has been practiced and realized by the third generation of Italian/American writers, the best of whom have met the challenge of experimenting with technique and style, and, in so doing, have carried their sense of *italianità* to new heights.

For the most part, the early Italian/American writers were dealing with contemporary subjects and themes which were based on autobiographical reflections of life in America. As we examine the later writers, the children and grandchildren of immigrants, we

---

[17] See her interview in *Fra Noi* (September 1986).

stage writer is the "pioneer spokesman for the . . . unspoken-for" ethnic, racial, or cultural group—the marginalized. This person writes about his/her co-others with the goal of dislodging and debunking negative stereotypes esconced in the dominant culture's mindset. In so doing, this writer may actually create characters possessing some of the very same stereotypes, with the specific goals, however, of 1) winning over the sympathies of the suspicious members of the dominant group, and 2) humanizing the stereotyped figure and thus "dissipating prejudice." Successful or not, this writer engages in placating his/her reader by employing recognizable features the dominant culture associates with specific ethnic, racial, or cultural groups.

Aaron considers this first-stage writer abjectly conciliatory toward the dominant group. He states: "It was as if he were saying to his suspicious and opinionated audience: 'Look, we have customs and manners that may seem bizarre and uncouth,

---

different generations that Joseph Lopreato (*Italian Americans* [New York: Random House, 1979]) and Paul Campisi ("Ethnic Family Patterns: The Italian Family in the United States" [*The American Journal of Sociology* 53.6 (May 1948)]) each describe and analyze: i.e., "peasant," "first-," "second-," and "third-generation." With regard to this fourth generation—Lopreato's and Campisi's "third generation"—I would state here, briefly, that I see the writer of this generation subsequent to Aaron's "third-stage writer," who eventually returns to his/her ethnicity through the process of re(dis)co-very. This notion of rediscovery will become more clear later in this essay, in the section ***The Non/Anglo/American Scene***.

but we are respectable people nevertheless and our presence adds flavor and variety to American life. Let me convince you that our oddities—no matter how quaint and amusing you find them—do not disqualify us from membership in the national family'."

What this writer seems to do, however, is engage in a type of game, a bartering system of sorts which ignores the injustices set forth by the dominant group, asking, or hoping, instead, that the very same dominant group might attempt to change its ideas while, at the same time, it accepts the writer's offerings as its final chance to enjoy the stereotype. The danger, of course, is, metaphorically speaking, of adding fuel to the fire, since there is no guarantee that such a strategy may convince the dominant culture to abandon its negative preconceptions and stereotypes.

Less willing to please, the second-stage writer, instead, abandons the use of preconceived ideas in an attempt to demystify negative stereotypes. Whereas the first-stage writer might have adopted some preconceived notions popular among members of the dominant culture, this writer, instead, presents characters who have already sunk "roots into the native soil." By no means therefore as conciliatory as the first-stage writer, this person readily indicates the disparity and, in some cases, may even engage in militant criticism of the perceived restrictions and oppression set forth by the dominant group. In so doing, according to Aaron, this writer runs the risk of a "double criticism": from the dominant culture offended by the "unflattering or even 'un-American' image of American life," as also from other members of his/her own marginalized group, who might feel misrepresented, having preferred a more "genteel and uncantankerous spokesman."

The third-stage writer, in turn, travels from the margin to the mainstream "viewing it no less critically, perhaps, but more knowingly." Having appropriated the dominant group's culture and tools necessary to succeed in that culture—the greater skill of manipulating, for instance, a language acceptable to the dominant group—and more strongly than his/her predecessors, this writer feels entitled to the intellectual and cultural heritage of the dominant group. As such, s/he can also, from a personal viewpoint, "speak out uninhibitedly as an American."[21] This writer, however, as Aaron reminds us, does not renounce or abandon the cultural heritage of his/her marginalized group. Instead, s/he transcends "a mere parochial allegiance" in order to transport "into the province of the [general] imagination," personal experiences which for the first-stage ("local colorist") and second-

[21]There are undoubtedly other considerations regarding Aaron's three categories. He goes on to discuss them further, providing examples from the Jewish and Black contingents of American writers.

stage ("militant protestor") writer comprised "the very stuff of their literary material."

One caveat with regard to this neat, linear classification of writers should not go unnoticed. There undoubtedly exists a clear distinction between the first-stage writer and the third-stage writer. The distinction, however, between the first- and second-stage writer, and especially that between the second- and third-stage writer, may at times seem blurred.[22] This becomes apparent when one discusses works such as Mario Puzo's *The Godfather* or Helen Barolini's *Umbertina*. More significant is the fact that these various stages of hyphenation may actually manifest themselves along the trajectory of one author's literary career. Helen Barolini, I would contend, manifests, to date, such a phenomenon. Her second novel, *Love in the Middle Ages*, revolves around a love story involving a middle-aged couple, whereas ethnicity and cultural origin serve chiefly as a backdrop.[23]

---

[22]In his rewrite, Aaron recognized the blurring of boundaries, as these "stages cannot be clearly demarcated" (13).

[23]Considering what Aaron states in his rewrite, and what seems to be of common opinion—that the respective experiences of Jews and Italians in the United States were similar in some says (23-24 especially)—it should appear as no strange coincidence, then, that the ethnic backgrounds of the two main characters are, for the woman, Italian, and, for the man, Jewish.

Turning now to Italian/American literature within the greater scheme of American letters, one sees that, until recently, very few have truly pondered the notion. For all practical purposes, Rose Basile Green's *The Italian-American Novel* bridged an initial, major gap between Italian/American narrative and the dominant group's notion of American literature. Underscoring the social and aesthetic values inherent in the various novels she includes in her book, Basile Green engages in a chronological analysis of Italian/American narrative.

Looking at literature from the semiotic perspective of sign production, on the other hand, William Boelhower published an important essay on the immigrant novel as genre.[24] Soon after, he published his *Immigrant Autobiography in the United States*,[25] which he followed two years later with his *Through a Glass Darkly*.[26] In this last book, Boelhower establishes the ethnic sign as, "above all an interpretive relation, a putting

---

[24]"The Immigrant Novel as Genre," *Melus* 8.1 [1981]: 3-14.

[25]*Immigrant Autobiography in the United States* (Venice, Italy: Essedue Edizioni, 1982).

[26]*Through a Glass Darkly: Ethnic Semiosis in American Literature* (Venice, Italy, Edizioni Helvetia, 1984: subsequently published in 1987 by Oxford University Press).

into relation," and not a series of "semantic correspondences."

Robert Viscusi, another of the few who have previously explored such a notion, recently engaged in a theoretical discussion on Italian/American literature.[27] As the "method that literature offers to deal with the cultural dissonance produced by his-torical process," allegory, for Viscusi, is a "communal work of art" through which a literature will eventually "define its own history." Surely, this is the case with the American writer of Italian descent, who, for many decades in this country, spoke *in other terms*, as might be said *allegorically*.[28]

Surely, American writers of Italian origin, as also other marginalized writers, do so from the perspective of *other*. This notion of *other* is undoubtedly the point of departure both for any emergent literature as also for any discourse developed around that literature, be it ethnic-, racial-, or gender-oriented. Thus, the autobiographical bent many see in the early works of the Italian/American writer, for example, surely represents the energy and early forms of the *allegory* such a literature and/or culture, in

---

[27] See his "A Literature Considering Itself: The Allegory of Italian America," in *From The Margin*: 265-81.

[28] In an etymological sense, *allegory* means, in fact, to "speak in *other* terms" (*The American Heritage Dictionary*; my emphasis).

Viscusi's terms, would develop in its quest for self-preservation.

In this case of a new allegory developed in an *other* literature's quest for self-preservation, concomitantly one also witnesses the decentralization of the "verbal-ideological world."[29] More specifically, along the lines of sign-functions, one sees that the two functives of expression and content are no longer in mutual correlation. The content, at this point in time with regard to an ethnic/ *other* literature, is different from that of the dominant culture. The sign-function realized in this new process of semiosis is now in disaccord with the dominant culture's expectation of the coding correlation.[30]

Another important consideration here is the interpreter's fore-understanding "drawn from [his/her] own anterior relation to the subject."[31] This notion of fore-understanding is, undoubtedly, a basis for both the sender's and the addressee's use and interpretation of signs. That is to say, the sign (or sign-function) is not ideologically neutral. Rather, its use and interpretation are dependent on both the sender's and addressee's

---

[29]See Mikhail M. Bakhtin, *The Dialogic Imagination*. Edited by Michael Holquist, translated by Caryl Emerson and Michael Holquist (Austin: U of Texas P, 1981): 258ff.

[30]For more on sign-functions, see Umberto Eco, *A Theory of Semiotics* (Bloomington: Indiana UP, 1976): 48-62.

[31]Hans-Georg Gadamer, *Truth and Method* (New York: The Crossroad Publishing Company, 1988): 262.

prejudgements.[32] In a general sense, then, language—its sign system—cannot be but ideologically invested. As an ideological medium, language can also become restrictive and oppressive when its sign system is arbitrarily invested with meanings by those who are empowered to do so—the dominant culture—for the purpose of privileging one coding correlation over an *other*, subjugating the *other* sign system to that of the dominant group, and, ultimately, denying validity to this *other* sign system.[33] Then, certain ideological constructs ("American" as in "American Literature") are privileged over others and subsequently awarded a fixed status; they take on a patina of *natural facts* rather than that of the *arbitrary categories* they truly are.

All this results in a monolithic notion of culture which, by its very nature, cannot include the individual who has found "a voice or style that does not violate [his/her] several

---

[32]For more on prejudgements see Gadamer 234-275.

[33]See, for example, V. N. Volosinov, *Marxism and the Philosophy of Language* trans. Ladislav Matejka and I. R. Titunik (Cambridge, MA: Harvard UP, 1986): "A sign does not simply exist as part of a reality—it reflects and refracts another reality. Therefore, it may distort that reality or be true to it, or may perceive it from a special point of view, and so forth. Every sign is subject to the criteria of ideological evaluation (whether it is true, false, correct, fair, good, etc.). The domain of ideology coincides with the domain of signs. They equate with one another. Wherever a sign is present ideology is present also. *Everything ideological possesses semiotic value.*"

components of identity" (Fischer), and who has thus (re)created, ideologically speaking, a different repertoire of signs. Nevertheless, the emergence and subsequent acceptance of certain *other* literatures, due in great part to the postmodern influence of the breakdown of boundaries and the mistrust in absolutes, has contributed to the construction of a more recent heteroglossic culture in which the "correct language" (Bakhtin) is deunified and decentralized. In this instance, then, all "languages" are shown to be "masks [and no language can consequently] claim to be an authentic and incontestable face." The result is a "heteroglossia consciously opposed to [the dominant] literary language," for which marginalization—and thus the silencing—of the *other* writer becomes more difficult to impose and thus less likely to occur.[34]

Turning now to a few writers, we see that their work represents to one degree or another the general notions and ideas outlined above. John Fante, Pietro Di Donato, and Joseph Tusiani—two fiction writers (Fante and Di Donato) and a poet (Tusiani)—

[34]This, for Bakhtin, is dialogized heteroglossia. A work, language, or culture undergoes dialogization "when it becomes relatived, depriviliged, aware of competing definitions for the same things." Only by "breaking through to its own meaning and own expression across an environ-ment full of alien words and variously evaluating accents, harmonizing with some of the elements in this environment and striking a dissonance with others, is [a word—or for that matter, language, or culture] able, in this dialogized process, to shape its own stylistic profile and tone."

have produced a corpus of writing heavily informed by their Italian heritage. Their works celebrate their ethnicity and cultural origin, as each weaves tales and creates verses which tell of the trials and tribulations of the Italian immigrants and their children. Fante and Di Donato confronted both the ethnic dilemma and the writer's task of communicating this dilemma in narrative form. Tusiani, on the other hand, invites his reader, through the medium of poetry, to understand better, as Giordano points out, the "cynical and somber awareness of what it means to be an immigrant," and to experience the "alienation and realization that the new world is not the 'land of hospitality' he/she believed it was."[35] So that, be it the novelist Di Donato, or the short-story writer Fante, Tusiani's "riddle of [his] day" figures indeed as the riddle of many of his generation, as it may also continue to sound a familiar chord for those of subsequent generations: "Two languages, two lands, perhaps two souls. . . / Am I a man or two strange halves of one?"[36]

In a cultural/literary sense, it becomes clear that these and other writers of their generation belong to what Aaron considers

[35]See Paolo A. Giordano, "From Southern Italian Immigrant to Reluctant American: Joseph Tusiani's *Gente Mia and Other Poems*" in *From the Margin*: 317.

[36]See his "Song of the Bicentennial (V)," in *Gente Mia and Other Poems* (Stone Park, IL: Italian Cultural Center, 1978).

stage one of the *hyphenate writer*. For this writer not only questions his/her origins, but, as mentioned above, is indeed bent on disproving the suspicions and prejudices of the dominant culture. Fante, Di Donato, and Tusiani, as also their *co/ethnics*, indeed both examined their status in the new world and, insofar as possible, presented a positive image of the Italian in America.

In turn, writers who have securely passed from the first through the second and onto the third stage of hyphenation may include the likes of Mario Puzo, Helen Barolini, and Gilbert Sorrentino. While it is true that each writer has dealt with his/her cultural heritage, each has done so both differently from each other as also from those who preceded them. No longer feeling the urge to please the dominant culture, these writers adopted the thematics of their Italian heritage insofar as it coincided with their personal development as writers.

Mario Puzo's second novel, *A Fortunate Pilgrim* (1964), recounts the trials and tribulations of a first-generation immigrant family. Ethnically centered around Lucia, the matriarch of the Corbo family, the novel examines the myth of the American dream and the real possibility of the *outsider* to succeed in realizing it. To be sure, Puzo, as he does later in the *The Godfather*, does not always paint a positive picture of the Italian American in this novel. Yet, considered from the perspective of a greater social criticism, Puzo's use of a sometimes sleazy, Italian/American character—especially those involved in the stereotypical organized crime associations—may figure as an indictment of the social dynamism of the dominant culture which refuses access to the *outsider*.[37] The novel's expansive theme of survival and the desire to better one's situation lies at the base of the variegated, kaleidoscopic view of a series of seemingly overwhelming tragedies which the family, as a whole, seems to overcome.

In considering another example, we see that Helen Barolini's *Umbertina* (1979) could not be more Italian American. The author of a novel which spans four generations of an Italian/American family, she is, undoubtedly, acutely aware of her ethnicity and hyphenation. Her main characters are all women, and each represents a different generation. In a general sense, they reflect the development of the Italian/American mindset as it evolved and changed from one generation to the next. Yet, with this novel, it becomes increasingly clear that Barolini has gone one step further than those who preceded her, both the men and women. In *Umbertina,* Barolini now combines her historical awareness of the Italian and Italian American's plight with her own strong sense of feminism, and, ulti-

---

[37]Basile Green expresses an analogous notion in her section on Puzo in *The Italian-American Novel.*

mately, the reader becomes aware of what it meant to be not just an Italian American but indeed an Italian/American woman.[38]

As John Paul Russo has demonstrated, Gilbert Sorrentino does attempt to fuse his inherited immigrant culture—which is represented by terms of nature in his poetry—with his artistic concern.[39] Yet, references to Italian/American culture are most infrequent throughout his *opus*. In his own words, Sorrentino surely "knew the reality of [his] generation that had to be written,"[40] as he too contributed to this cultural and literary chronicle. However, he took one step further than his *co/ethnics* (Italian Americans) and, so to speak, dropped the hyphen. Yet the dropping of the hyphen, according to Aaron, does not necessarily eliminate a writer's

---

[38]For more on the gender/ethnic dilemma in *Umbertina*, see my "Helen Barolini's *Umbertina*: The Ethnic/Gender Dilemma," in *Italian Americans Celebrate Life: The Arts and Popular Culture*. Edited by Paola A. Sensi-Isolani and Anthony Julian Tamburri (Staten Island, NY: The American Italian Historical Association, 1990): 29-44; for a larger version of this essay dealing also with the intertwining themes of ethnic and gender dilemma in *Umbertina*, see my "*Umbertina*: The Italian/American Woman's Experience," in *From the Margin*: 357-73..

As already mentioned, in her later novel, *Love in the Middle Ages*, the subject matter is much more universal insofar as ethnicity and cultural origin are backdrops to a love story involving a middle-aged couple.

[39]See Russo's essay, "The Poetics of Gilbert Sorrentino," *Rivista di Studi Anglo-Americani* 3 (1984-85): 281-303.

[40]*Vort* 2 (1974): 19. I owe this quote to John Paul Russo, "The Poetics of Gilbert Sorrentino."

marginality. He states that the writer ". . . has detached himself, to be sure, from one cultural environment without becoming a completely naturalized member of the official environment. It is not so much that he retains a divided allegiance but that as a writer, if not necessarily as a private citizen, he has transcended a mere parochial allegiance and can now operate freely in the republic of the spirit." In Sorrentino's case, while he was keenly aware of the American literary tradition that preceded him, in dropping the ethnic hyphen he appropriated yet another form of marginality; with the likes of Kerouac and Ferlinghetti as immediate predecessors, Sorrentino chose the poetics of late Modernism over that of mainstream literary America.[41]

---

[41] Again, I refer the reader to John Paul Russo's "The Poetics of Gilbert Sorrentino."

The Hyphen

Hyphen-nation

Sitting atop the hyphen provides a marvelous view, but no
direction.
Does one face forward or backward? Look behind or ahead?
the hyphen is incomplete; there is no where to go.
the force of the dash,
the inclusiveness of the parenthesis,
the finality of the period.
The Hyphen only supports. It does not connect.

Japanese-American, Mexican-American, Italian-American—
Lacking the two slight marks that gives the arrow its
certainty,
the hyphen is incomplete; there is no where to go.
Existing between two cultures, it is an eternal bridge
with barriers and guards at both ends.[42]

In a previous section, we read that the hyphen initially represented the dominant group's reluctance to accept the new/comer. It was the group's way, Aaron stated, of holding the new/comer "at 'hyphen's length,' so to speak, from the established community." Drawing on what Aaron had originally expressed in the early version of his essay on the hyphenate writer and what Marshall Grossman more recently stated in his essay, "The Violence of the Hyphen in Judeo-Christian," with specific regard to the presence of the

---

[42]Wendell Aycock, written on the occasion of a lecture during the Ninth Annual Comparative Literature Symposium, "Ethnic Literature Since 1776: The Many Voices of America," 1976; quoted in *Melus* 7.1 (1980): 2.

hyphen,[43] I contend that the hyphen is much more of a disjunctive element, rather than a conjunctive one, when used in couplets denoting national origin, ethnicity, race, or gender. It is, to be sure, a colonializing sign that hides its ideological and, therefore, subjugating force under the guise of grammatical correctness.[44]

What is problematical about a discussion on the hyphen is that it depends on grammatical exigencies which require its presence in certain situations; I refer to the adjectival couplet mentioned above. A significant dilemma concerning the arbitrary dropping of the hyphen—my replacing it with the slash in this essay—manifests itself when, instead, the hyphen is required by still another arbitrary, though already legitimized, decision; i.e., a grammar rule, or what I consider (as evident at the outset of this essay) one of many arbitrary constructs set up by those who are empowered to do so. Recalling again what Aaron had subsequently stated about the hyphen—that the hyphen further "signifies a tentative but unmistakable withdrawal" on the user's part, so that "mere geographical proximity" denies the newly arrived "full and

---

[43]Marshall Grossman, "The Violence of the Hyphen in Judeo-Christian," *Social Text* 22 (Spring 1989): 115-122.

[44]Indeed, from an etymological standpoint, the hyphen may also be considered an obliterating diacritical mark. According to *The American Heritage Dictionary* the hyphen has its origin in "*hupo-*, under + *hen*, neuter of *heis*, one." Thus it has its roots in domination and subjugation.

unqualified national membership *despite . . . legal qualifications and . . . official disclaimers to the contrary*" (my emphasis)—we see that the situation becomes increasingly problematical. What occurs, to borrow from Grossman's essay, is that an "ideological structure . . . enters . . . political discourse through a profoundly linguistic formation"—the hyphen—which, in turn, sets up an "internalized hierarchy between one identification and its syncretic sequel, [for which] *the hyphen asserts the addition of a second term without the erasure of the first, in a way that preserves the original term as the mark of its difference from itself*." The hyphen, that is, takes on the sign-function of separateness—"the original term as the mark of its difference from itself"—and virtually underscores the difference perceived in the first group (the "original term"). It keeps the "original term" (the ethnic group) at "hyphen's length" (the dominant group's reluctance to grant "full and unqualified national membership" to the ethnic group) despite other arbitrary constructs which signify otherwise—"legal qualifications and . . . official disclaimers to the contrary." That is to say, a type of ideological chiasmus, disguised by homonymy, seems to develop in this situation: as if the dominant culture were saying to the ethnic group, *Of course, we're all Americans, but there are Americans and then there are Americans*, in which case the signifer, "Americans," figures as a polyvalent term whose various signifieds can be utilized or discarded according to the exigenices of the situation.

I would, moreover, contend that the hyphen manifests its disjunctive characteristic in other ways. As we have seen above, it underscores the ideological difference perceived in the "original term": that is, it sets up a contrast between the ethnic and the dominant groups from the perspective of the latter. In addition, the separateness caused by the hyphen is physically manifested. The hyphen, that is, actually creates space—a physical gap—when (and where), instead, space—an ideological gap—should be readily filled.[45] Graphically depicted, we have:

Italian—American

Keeping this short graphic in mind, it should become clear at this point that the substitution of the slash for the hyphen is not necessarily the *removal* of one diacritical mark by another, as may have been the reader's initial inference at the opening of this essay. Instead, my suggestion to adopt the slash in place of the hyphen involves not *removing* the hyphen but, more precisely,

---

[45]Lest we ignore the previous, more popular hyphenated phrase, *Italo-American*, where the first term is undoubtedly a violation of the complete form of the adjective, *Italian*. In this regard, Victoria J. R. DeMara has brought up in conversation the notion of such violation as, virtually, an act of *castration*.

tilting it on its end by forty-five degrees, as depicted below:

Italian—American —> Italian/American

Such a prestidigitatious maneuver accomplishes two things. In the first case, it actually bridges the physical gap between the two terms, thus bringing them closer together. Indeed, the greater physical vicinity, if it has any ideological function at all, should aid in closing the ideological gap. Secondly, the integrity of the grammatical rule requiring a grapheme between two such terms in an adjectival phrase would remain intact. This, in turn, would undoubtedly muffle any disapproving clamors possibly provoked by what some may consider an affront to grammatical exigencies of the English language.

A Tentative Conclusion

In dealing with his/her Italian/American inheritance, each writer picks up something different as s/he may perceive and interpret his/her cultural heritage filtered through personal experiences. Yet, there resounds a familiar ring, an echo that connects them all. Undoubtedly, Italian/American writers have slowly, but surely, built their niche in the body of American literature. Collectively, their work can be viewed as a written expression par excellence of Italian/American culture; individually, each writer has enabled American literature to sound a slightly different tone, thus bringing to the fore another voice of the great kaleidoscopic, socio/cultural mosaic we may call Americana—*kaleidoscopic mosaic* precisely because the socio/cultural dynamics of the United States reveal a constant flux of changes originating in the very existence of the various differentiated ethnic/racial groups that constitute the overall population of the United States.

On this note, then, I would state that a possible response to the question in my title—"To Hyphenate Or Not To Hyphenate?"—can be found through an intertextual rereading, a process similar to what Boelhower has called an "inferencing context."[46] For it is the

---

[46]*Through a Glass Darkly*, 38.

reader's task to reconcile the textual offerings with his/her cultural reservoir of knowledge. In so doing, s/he should succeed in bringing closer together, as Viscusi states, "that large intersection of scripture and interpretation which goes by the name *allegoresis*." As a result, then, s/he is ultimately one step closer to perceiving the "cultural dissonance produced by historical process." In like manner, Fischer has stated that "[w]hat emerges is not simply that parallel processes operate across American ethnic identities, but a sense that these ethnic identities *constitute only a family of resemblances*, that ethnicity cannot be reduced to identical sociological functions, that ethnicity is a process of *inter-reference between two or more cultural traditions*" (my emphasis).

Thus, perhaps, an appropriate way to close would be to borrow again from both Grossman and Lyotard. For if the "power of the [hyphen, as Grossman states] lies in its openness to history [, or, better still,] in the way it records and then reifies contingent events," since the "ideology of a particular hyphen may be read only by supplying a plausible history to its use," the person who opts to eliminate it, to use something else in its place, or, as I have ultimately suggested, turn it on its side, does so in the search "for new presentations," to quote now from Lyotard. In this manner, then, the text the writer creates, the work s/he "produces are not in principle governed by preestablished rules [i.e., canon formation], and they cannot be judged according to a determining judgement, by applying familiar categories to the text or to the work. Those rules and categories are what the work of art is looking for. The artist and the writer, then, are working without rules in order to formulate the rules of what *will have been done*" (emphasis textual).

In an analogous manner, so does the reader of these same texts work without rules, establishing, as s/he proceeds similar interpretive rules of what *will have been read*. Such is the case with the reader of *ethnic* texts, who proceeds to recodify and reinterpret the seemingly arbitrary—non-canonical (read also *ethnic*)—signs in order to reconstruct a mutual correlation of the expressive and content functives, which, in the end, do not violate his/her intertextual knowledge. Moreover, such an act of semiosis relies on the individual's time and place, and is therefore always new and different with respect to its own historical specificities vis-à-vis the dominant culture—the canon.

It is, in final analysis, a dynamics of the conglomeration and agglutination of different voices and reading strategies which, contrary to the hegemony of the dominant culture, cannot be fully integrated into any strict semblance of a monocultural voice or process of interpretation. The utterance, therefore, will always be polyvalent, its combination will always be rooted in heteroglossia and dialogism,[47] and the interpretive strategies for decoding it will always depend on the specificities of the reader's intertextual reservoir.

West Lafayette, Indiana (USA)
December 1990

[47]For more on the notions of heteroglossia and dialogism, see Bakhtin, *The Dialogic Imagination:* 426, 428 passim.

Bibliography

Aaron, Daniel, "The Hyphenate Writer and American Letters," *Smith Alumnae Quarterly* (July 1964): 213-7; later revised for *Rivista di Studi Anglo-Americani* 3.4-5 (1984-85): 11-28.

Ahmad, Aijaz, "Jameson's Rhetoric of Otherness and the 'National Allegory'," *Social Text* 17 (1987): 3-25.

Altieri, Charles, "An Idea and Ideal of a Literary Canon," *Canons*, ed. Robert von Hallberg. Chicago: University Chicago Press, 1984: 41-64.

Aycock, Wendell, "Hyphen-nation," *MELUS* 7.1 (1980): 2.

Bakhtin, Mikhail M. *The Dialogic Imagination*. Edited by Michael Holquist, translated by Caryl Emerson & Michael Holquist. Austin: University of Texas Press, 1981.

Barolini, Helen, "Introduction," *The Dream Book. An Anthology of Writings by Italian American Women*. New York: Schoken, 1985.

___. "Interview," in *Fra Noi* (September 1986).

Boelhower, William, "The Immigrant Novel as Genre," *Melus* 8.1 (1981): 3-14.

___. *Immigrant Autobiography in the United States*. Venice, Italy: Essedue Edizioni, 1982.

___. *Through a Glass Darkly: Ethnic Semiosis in American Literature*. Venice, Italy, Edizioni Helvetia, 1984: subsequently published in 1987 by Oxford University Press.

Bona, Mary Jo, "Mari Tomasi's *Like Lesser Gods*: The Making of an Ethnic *Bildungsroman*," *Voices in Italian Americana* 1.1 (1990): 15-34.

Brennan, Timothy ed. *Modern Fiction Studies* 35.1 (1989).

Caetura, Linda, ed, *Growing Up Italian*. New York: Morrow & Co., 1985.

Campisi, Paul, "Ethnic Family Patterns: The Italian Family in the United States," *The American Journal of Sociology* 53.6 (May 1948).

Caroli, Betty Boyd, Robert F. Harney, and Lydio F. Tomasi, eds. *The Italian Immigrant Woman in North America*. Toronto: The Multicultural History Society in Ontario, 1978.

Eco, Umberto. *A Theory of Semiotics*. Bloomington: Indiana University Press, 1976.

Firmat, Gustavo Pérez, "Spic Chic: Spanglish as Equipment for Living," *The Caribbean Review* 15.3 (Winter 1987): 20ff.

Fischer, Michael M. J., "Ethnicity and the Post-Modern Arts of Memory," in *Writing Culture. The Poetics and Politics of Ethnography*. Edited by James Clifford & George E. Marcus. Berkeley; University of California Press, 1986).

Gadamer, Hans-Georg. *Truth and Method*. New York: The Crossroad Publishing Company, 1988.

Gardaphé, Fred, "Italian/American Fiction: A Third-Generation Renaissance," *MELUS* 14.3-4 (1987): 69-85.

Giordano, Paolo A., "From Southern Italian Immigrant to Reluctant American: Joseph Tusiani's *Gente Mia and Other Poems*" in *From the Margin: Writings in Italian Americana*. Anthony Julian Tamburri, Paolo A. Giordano, & Fred L. Gardaphé, editors. West Lafayette, IN: Purdue University Press, 1991: 316-28.

Green, Rose Basile. *The Italian-American Novel: A Document of the Interaction of Two Cultures*. Madison, NJ: Fairleigh Dickinson University Press, 1974.

Grossman, Marshall, "The Violence of the Hyphen in Judeo-Christian," *Social Text* 22 (1989): 115-22.

Jameson, Frederic, "Third World Literature in an Era of Multinational Capitalism," *Social Text* 15 (1986).

Katrek, Ketu H. "Decolonializing Culture: Toward a Theory for Postcolonial Women's Text," *Modern Fiction Studies* 35.1.

Lopreato, Joseph. *Italian Americans.* New York: Random House, 1979.

Lyotard, Jean-François. *The Postmodern Condition: A Report on Knowledge,* trans. Geoff Bennington & Brian Massumi with a foreword by Frederic Jameson. Minneapolis: University of Minnesota Press, 1984.

Ohmann, Richard, "The Shaping of a Canon: U.S. Fiction, 1960-1975," *Canons,* ed. Robert von Hallberg. Chicago: University of Chicago Press, 1984; 377-402.

Parini, Jay, "Interview," *Fra Noi* (April 1987).

Rimanelli, Giose, "Introduction," *Modern Canadian Studies.* Toronto: Reyerson Press, 1966.

Russo, John Paul, "The Poetics of Gilbert Sorrentino," *Rivista di Studi Anglo-Americani* 3 (1984-85): 281-303.

Sensi-Isolani, Paola A. & Anthony Julian Tamburri, eds.*Italian Americans Celebrate Life: The Arts and Popular Culture.* Staten Island, NY: American Italian Historical Association, 1990.

Tamburri, Anthony Julian, "Helen Barolini's *Umbertina*: The Ethnic/Gender Dilemma," in *Italian Americans Celebrate Life: The Arts and Popular Culture.* Edited by Paola A. Sensi-Isolani & Anthony Julian Tamburri. Staten Island, NY: American Italian Historical Association, 1990: 29-44.

___. "*Umbertina*: The Italian/American Woman's Experience," in *From the Margin: Writings in Italian Americana.* Anthony Julian Tamburri, Paolo A. Giordano, and Fred L. Gardaphé, editors. West Lafayette, IN: Purdue UP, 1991: 357-73.

Tamburri, Anthony Julian, Paolo A. Giordano & Fred L. Gardaphé, eds. *From the Margin: Writ-*

ings in Italian Americana. West Lafayette, IN: Purdue UP, 1991.

Tusiani, Joseph, "Song of the Bicentennial (V)," in *Gente Mia and Other Poems.* Stone Park, IL: Italian Cultural Center, 1978.

Valesio, Paolo, "The Writer Between Two Worlds: The Italian Writer in the United States," *DIFFERENTIA* 3/4 (Spring/Autumn 1989): 259-76.

Viscusi, Robert, "A Literature Considering Itself: The Allegory of Italian America," in *From The Margin. Writings in Italian Americana.* Anthony Julian Tamburri, Paolo A. Giordano, & Fred L. Gardaphé, editors. West Lafayette, IN: Purdue UP, 1991: 265-81.

Volosinov, V. N. *Marxism and the Philosophy of Language* trans. Ladislav Matejka & I. R. Titunik. Cambridge, MA: Harvard UP, 1986.

Index

Aaron, Daniel , 28-32, 41-42, 43, 44.
African/American fiction, 19.
Ahmad, Aijaz, 16-17.
Altieri, Charles, 19, n. 10.
Anglo/American culture, 19.
Ardizzone, Tony, 20.
Atlantic Monthly, 22.
Aycock, Wendell, 43, n. 42.
Bakhtin, Mikhail M., 35-36, 37, 37, n. 34.
Barolini, Helen, 9, n. 2, 25, n. 16, 26, 32, 39, 40-41.
Black Americans, 12, n. 3.
Boelhower, William, 33-34, 48.
Bona, Mary Jo, 25, n. 16.
Brennan, Timothy, 9, n. 2.
Campisi, Paul, 28, n. 20.
canon, 19, n. 10, 50.
canon valorization , 19.
Caroli, Betty Boyd, Robert F. Harney, and Lydio F. Tomasi, eds. *The Italian Immigrant Woman in North America*, 25, n. 16.
Cassettari, Rosa, 26, 27.
Christ in Concrete, 26.
Ciardi, John, 22-23.
Corso, Gregory, 25.
Cultural Critique, 9, n. 2.
DeMara, Victoria J. R., 46, n. 45.
dialogism, 51.
dialogization, 37, n. 34.
Di Donato, Pietro, 24, 25, n. 16, 26, 37-39.
di Prima, Diane, 24, 27.
dominant culture/group, 12, n. 4, 13, 15, 19, 29-31, 36-40, 43, 50.
dominant-group critics, 2.
The Dream Book. An Anthology of Writings by Italian American Women, 9, n. 2.
Eco, Umberto, 35, n. 30.

English language, 17, 17, n. 8.
ethnic, 22.
ethnic recovery (also, re[dis]covery), 20-21, 28, n. 20.
ethnic studies/literature, 12-14, 16.
ethnic writers, 22.
ethnicity, 20-22, 28, n. 20, 33, 40, 41, n. 38, 49.
Ets, Marie Hall, 26.
Fante, John, 24, 25, n. 16, 27, 37-39.
feminism, 40-41.
Ferlinghetti, Lawrence, 25, 42.
Firmat, Gustavo Pérez, 9, n. 2.
Fischer, Michael M. J., 20-21, 36-37, 49.
A Fortunate Pilgrim, 39.
Gadamer, Hans-Georg, 35-36.
Gardaphé, Fred, 9, n. 1, 27, n. 18.
Gioia, Dana, 20.
Giordano, Paolo A., 9, n. 1, 38.
The Godfather (novel), 32, 39.
grammar (rules), 17-18, 44-47.
Green, Rose Basile, 28, n. 19, 33, 40, n. 37.
Grossman, Marshall, 43-45, 49.
Hallberg, Robert von, 19, n. 10.
heteroglossia, 37, 37, n. 34, 51.
hyphen, 10-11, 17-18, 41, 43-47.
hyphenate writer, 11, 28-32, 38-42.
  first-stage, 28-30, 32, 38-42.
  second-stage, 30-31, 32, 38-42.
  third-stage, 31-32, 38-42.
hyphenation (also, dehyphenation), 28-32, 38-42.
"Hyphen-nation", 43.
Immigrant Autobiography in the United States, 33.
intertextuality (intertextual recall), 10, 13, 48, 50-51.
Italian/American family, 39, 40.
The Italian-American Novel: A Document of the Interaction of Two Cultures, 33.
Italian/American literature, 33-42.
Italian/American writers, 20-27, 25, n. 16 (female), 48.

Italian Identity in America (see also, *italianità*), 20-23.
The Italian Journal, 9 n. 1.
Italian writer in the United States, 9, n. 2.
italianità, 20-22, 24-27.
Italo-American, 46, n. 45.
Italy, 22.
Jameson, Frederic, 14-16.
Jewish/American fiction, 19.
Katrek, Ketu H., 14-15.
Kerouac, Jack, 42.
Left Curve, 9, n. 2.
Lopreato, Joseph, 28, n. 20.
Love in the Middle Ages, 32, 41, n. 38.
Lowell, Robert, 22-23.
Lyotard, Jean-François, 18-19, 49-50.
Mangione, Jerre, 24.
Marotta, Kenny, 20.
Modern Fiction Studies, 9. n. 2.
modernism, 42.
Mussolini, Benito, 22.
nationalism/nationalist ideologies, 14-16.
Native Americans, 12, n.3.
Ohmann, Richard, 19, n. 10.
other, 34-37.
other literature, 13, 34-37.
otherness, 16.
outsider, 39-40.
Parini, Jay, 20, 27.
The Patch Boys, 20.
postcolonial women, 14.
postcolonial societies, 14.
postmodern(ism), 18-19, 49-50.
pluriculturalism, 9, 16.
Puzo, Mario, 32, 39-40.
Raptosh, Diane, 20.
reader (interpreter), 10, 29, 35-37, 42, 48-51.
Rimanelli, Giose, 25, n. 16.

Ruffolo, Lisa, 20.
Russo, John Paul, 41-42.
semiosis, 33-37, 50-51.
semiotics, 33-34, 36, n. 33.
signs, 33-37, 36, n. 33, 50-51.
  interpretation of, 35-36.
  sign-function, 33-37, 45-46.
  sign production, 33-37.
slash, 10-11, 17, 44, 46.
Sorrentino, Gilbert, 39, 41-42.
South Atlantic Quarterly, 9, n. 2.
Stefanile, Felix, 25.
Tamburri, Anthony Julian, 9, n. 1, 41, n. 38.
Telos, 9, n. 2.
third-world, 14-17.
Through a Glass Darkly: Ethnic Semiosis in American Literature, 33.
Tusiani, Joseph, 25, .37-39.
Umbertina, 32, 40-41.
Valesio, Paolo, 9, n. 2, 20, n. 12.
Viscusi, Robert, 34-35, 49.
Volosinov, V. N., 36, n. 33.

Anthony Julian Tamburri is an associate professor of Italian at Purdue University. He has written *Of **Saltimbanchi** and **Incendiari**: Aldo Palazzeschi and Avant-Gardism in Italy* (Fairleigh Dickinson University Press, 1990) and has recently completed another book entitled, *Per una lettura retrospettiva. Prose giovanili di Aldo Palazzeschi* (forthcoming). He is one of the co-founding editors of *Voices in Italian Americana, a literary and cultural review (VIA)*; a contributing coeditor of the anthology *From the Margin: Writings in Italian Americana* (Purdue University Press, 1991); and cofounder of the Purdue Conference on Romance Languages, Literatures & Film and the *Romance Languages Annual*.

Finished printed
in August 1991 on presses
from Ateliers Graphiques Marc Veilleux Inc.
Cap-Saint-Ignace, Qué.